WE'LL NEVER HAVE PARIS

editor and cover designer
ANDRIA ALEFHI and JAIME BORSCHUK
interior drawings and photographs
LABELED BY ARTIST
typography and layout design
VERONICA STAEHLE

Donuts at Home

(From my blog donutsathome.blogspot.com)

ive in Manhattan, try to
ublish a zine and stave off
eneral insanity.

SATURDAY, NOVEMBER 17, 2007
●●● sold—first copy of my own zine

I finally decided to print my own collection of writings. This publication, zine, journal, book is not called donuts at home. Its called We'll never have Paris. Volume I.

I just came back from the copy shop. I wanted to print it myself and couldn't deal with it. I'm very pleased with how it came out on ivory paper and all. This volume contains 5 pieces. Today I sold my first copy. She bought it for a friend who loves Paris. I informed her that the stories had nothing to do with Paris. I like to be honest. She said that was all right.

Contact me if you'd like a copy. Free to regular readers. I know who you are. Three dollars to everyone else, or else, a barter. We'll never have Paris. I'm ready to start bringing it to indie bookshops and cafes. If you want to submit an essay for volume II, email an essay to me. Spread the word.

Posted by neverhaveparis at 3:45 PM

Labels: contribute, diy, donuts at home, journals, NYC, we'll never have paris, zines

PLEASE ENJOY THIS COLLECTION,
We'll Never Have Paris Greatest Hits: selections from Volumes 1-8.

SUBMISSION CRITERIA
FOR WNHP HAS BEEN

that it is a true story in memoir form about **all things never meant to be.**

volume

1	Fiction Once Removed	Fall 2007
2	Fictional Nonfiction	Spring 2008
3	Narrative Nonfiction Nanoseconds	Fall 2008
4	We are all telling the truth	Spring 2009
5	Home	Fall 2009
6	Now With Poetry	Spring 2010
7	Modern Fire	Fall 2010
8	Rejection	Spring 2011

- **MARGUERITE DABAIE** 7 *digital rot*
- **MARTHA GROVER** 3 at the cheese counter
- **MATTHEW MENDEZ** 4 folds
- **KAREN LILLIS** 5 migraines, tornados, fire-eaters, and other mysteries
- **RUSS JOSEPHS** 2 i was a scientologist
- **REDGUARD** 3 between here and there
- **TIFFANY STEVENS** 2 mr.big
- **JAIME BORSCHUK** 6 please don't confront me
- **ERIC NELSON** 6 young, dumb and full of ink
- **JOSH MEDSKER** 8 my name
- **BETSY HOUSTEN** 7 motel show
- **CECELIA MARISCAL** 5 submission
- **LAUREN NICOLE NIXON** 7 *flash narrative*
- **GUS IVERSEN** 5 different directions
- **ADITI SRIRAM** 6 taking direction from a sunset
- **ANDRIA ALEFHI** 1 musical mondays
- **DAVE COLE** 3 jerkface
- **CYNTHIA BALL** 8 the lamb store

MARTHA GROVER
AT THE CHEESE COUNTER

"I'm looking for an entry level goat cheese,"
The man says to me. He has some flour tortillas and a couple of chicken breasts in his shopping cart. He looks worried.

I wonder what an *"entry level goat cheese"* is. I know what a goat is. I know what cheese is. Goat cheese is the result of a process. It's what happens when grass interacts with a goat, its hormones, a farmer, mold and time. It's what happens when a bodily fluid is exposed to extremes in temperature, to centuries-old tradition and the market economy. Goat cheese is the result of an accident eons ago when early herding cultures started milking their goats and left some of the milk in a leather sack overnight, hanging from the eve of their hut, or in the corner of their cave. Goat cheese is what happens when you age the goat's milk, then wrap it in wax, in leaves, or esophageal tubing. I know what this is.

But what is entry level—the point at which you enter? Where the grass enters mouths, stomachs, udders? Is it where the milk enters the world, hot and steaming from the teat? Is it where I enter the grocery store, enter my employee number into the time clock and don my hat, name tag and apron? Is the entry level where the wire enters the cheese, splitting it in two? Is it where the cheese enters the plastic wrap, and gets entered into the scale at 15.99 a pound? Is entry level the place where I spend eight hours a day cutting, wrapping, weighing and pricing the bodily fluid of an animal, this cheese, the result of a process that begins and ends with digestion, that begins with the earth and ends with the earth? Is it where I package my own bodily fluids, my blood, sweat and tears into eight hour shifts, ten minute breaks and two week pay–periods?

I look at the man, his face impatient, eager to suck at the teat of my vast cheese knowledge. I feel like telling him that every entry level is also an exit level. That all hierarchy is an illusion. That he should follow his heart. Instead I recommend the Goat Gouda, the Goat Jack or if he wants something saltier, the Murcia Curado.

He thanks me and chooses the Goat Jack.

Matthew Mendez
FOLDS

Today it rained and I took the BMX bike I got for my sixteenth birthday from the garage to the basement, where I set it upside down in the doorway below the pull-up bar. I sat on the front wheel and it nestled nicely between my butt cheeks, reminding me of my grandfather's joke about the functional benefit of burying a person *"ass up;"* doing so creates a perfect place to park a bicycle. I laughed and peddled for twenty minutes. I was uncomfortable, bored, and embarassed, but i had to laugh; it was funny.

I did this because slowly, so slow that I didn't even notice when it began, but certain as a bullet, I am gaining weight. It sits in my center like a knot in a string. When I sit it folds and frowns upon me. I need to start working out.

Of course I've never been attractive. I lead a librarian's life, have a librarian's body, and keep a catalogue—Dewey Decimal; I'll never go LC —of dissatisfaction at my own appearance: poor posture; lack of muscle tone; unwanted hair on my belly, around my nipples; want of hair on my face; acne; back acne, or *"bacne;"* chest acne, or *"chacne;"* broken, crooked, yellow teeth. But what I obsess over the most, perhaps because I could potentially do something about it, is the growing tumor between my chest and genitals.
I need to start working out.

I bore my friends with talk of these insecurities and they show me hostility. Eric let me think I was going bald because he was sick of reassuring me. Alex yelled at me after I overfished the compliment pond. My whining, I'm sure, is less attractive than any physical shortcoming, but I need the solace of another's kind words. I need to start working out. I told my best friend.

> *"Like at the gym?"* he asked.
>
> *"Yeah,"* I said.
>
> *"Fuck that."* He said.

And thus the basement, where I've been doing all the ups: push sit pull, up up up. I've been trying to get my blessed, fat-burning cardio in the great outdoors, but today it rained and I brought my bike inside, where I remembered exactly why I don't exercise: I hate it. Sweaty and out of breath, and INSIDE, no less, is no way to go through one's days. The same could be said of shallow preoccupation, I know.

My first love was an athlete and she was tight allover. When we were alone I could squeeze her buttocks and taut tissue would push back to encourage my lecherous hands. I thought all asses must feel like that. Had I ever grabbed my own I would have realized that wasn't the case. My first love once said she loved my little body, once, but frequently complained of my disinterest in sport, frequently. My first love dumped me and I fell into my second as if a depression, a girl so soft she seemed a liquid, retained by a membrane of freckles and Psoriasis. I hated touching her and we broke up. She's a mother now. The first doesn't want children; she worries they'll ruin her figure.

You can find a new philosophy anywhere if you're open to it. *"Fuck that,"* mantra of the disaffected, can be reassuring, empowering, when the right person says it to you. I tried to date a girl in worse shape than I, and as I moaned at her like a moron about my proliferating bulb, she countered that she was gaining weight herself but could shrug it off; she liked drinking more than being thin. I suppose that's debased, but it struck me as serene. The night was a romantic disappointment and I haven't seen her since, but she gave me something better than a boner: an epiphany on the virtue of feeling good. We are here to be happy, aren't we?

I can overcome obsessions and anxieties, remind myself how inconsequential my slopes and sags really are, but I still waste hours by the quarter, standing in front of a mirror, sucking it in, standing up straight, jiggling and poking and pulling and propping, up up up. I'm fascinated by this flab. I try to flex and I embarrass myself, and then I recite the mantra. Fuck it. Whatever.

Up up up.

I like to read and I like to write. I stay seated and I grow hunched. Soft, pale and satisfied. If the weather's nice tomorrow I'll go outside and I'll ride my bike. I'll get wind in my hair, time with my thoughts, and a sense of accomplishment. My stomach will come along and he'll still be with me when I get home, hovering loyally above my waist, waiting for snacks, beer, and acceptance.

We share these goals, he and I.

Redguard
BETWEEN HERE AND THERE

Walking back to the train
from an East Village underground club.
It's after midnight. It's cold. I'm almost 37.

I feel swallowed by the darkness of deep
Alphabet City side streets, the broken
sidewalks under my steel-tipped riot boots,
the shadows and rats skittering past bent
lawn chairs in late winter's chill.

My mind races, drunk, but not from
alcohol. From being awake past twelve,
in the company of people, some known,
some strangers, branded by smoke and
chatter and the strong voice and crashing
cymbals of a favorite band.

I feel the pressure of sleep behind the
eyes. The sick feeling in my stomach, like
the one you get if you spend more than
a few minutes breathing the polyester
and plastic recycled air in Kmart.

I have a terrible desire to crumple onto
the sidewalk and never get up. That's
what happens when I remember: these
little moments are all I'll ever get.

Thinking of the Goth queen I danced
close with tonight. She was revered back
in the day and has only grown more

seductive with the years, she is still loved
by the scene but no longer enflames hearts,
minds and loins like she once did when
she was young and thin and smooth, and
I can't understand why.

When the DJ was spinning Andi Sexgang
and she was dancing so close, the electricity
flowed between us, and I could see her
making love to me, my hands glowing
on her tattooed back.

I want to worship in her temple and I don't
just mean that as a sexual metaphor and
then the song ends and the dance ends and
I am walking alone in the cold and it is
six months later and I am writing about it.

I will always be writing about it.

But I will get up in the morning, make
coffee, help my kid get dressed for school,
go to work, and use tonight as creativity fuel.

Never once
losing the
hollow feeling
in my gut.

Karen Lillis
MIGRAINES, TORNADOS, FIRE-EATERS, AND OTHER MYSTERIES

There was the migraine headache that came out of the blue

> when I'd gone to visit my brother and stood two hours in the blazing summer sun (on the banks of the James River) helping him deliberate over the potential purchase of a mini-kayak. After leaving Scottsville, I was due to drive back to my hometown, where my mother was waiting for me; after dinner with her, I had plans with my ex-high school sweetheart. Running late, it was getting less likely I could do both, but I was going to hear it from my mother if I skipped her part of the evening on a short visit "home" from New York.

"Home" was a pretty straight shot on just two sparsely travelled highways. Now the sun had ducked behind some clouds; I put on the radio, put the pedal to the metal and hoped to make good time. Not long into my drive, however, a radio announcement cut into my music to say that a tornado was making its way across central

> Virginia. I thought I heard something about Culpeper before the station went static, or was it Fredericksburg, and which way was it headed?

I kept hitting the search button on the radio dial,
but I could pick up nothing—all the radio stations
were out or barely audible— this wasn't the message
I wanted to hear.

I didn't know which path to follow—should I
pull over somewhere and get out of harm's way?
Or should I speed even faster towards home, because
my mother was going to kill me if I didn't get
there in time for dinner? There didn't seem room
to make a correct decision. I kept speeding on and
wondering, letting the fifth-gear driving be my
non-answer. I really didn't know what was the best
idea. I was terrified of getting smashed by a tornado
and equally terrified of causing my mother's
disappointment. My temples pounded.

I reached my parents' house
>   before the tornado
>   sent me to Oz, but
>   once there, I was
>   good for nothing.

The migraine was full-force, I had to cancel with
the ex, I went to bed instead of dinner. My mother
was furious, saying,

"You always get sick when you come home."

>   Another time,
>   I was living in Brooklyn.

A friend, Liz, was coming to the city from
Philadelphia to see the Bindlestiff Family Cirkus
perform in Williamsburg;
we were to meet up there

and she would come home
and sleep on my couch for
the night. I was excited to see the Cirkus because
I never had. Also, a friend was one of the founders:
my friend Stephanie had worked with me on the
Paper Floor at Pearl Paint, back when she had
spiky short hair and I had a bob. Stephanie
worked in the Roll aisle and I had moved from
the Paper Sheet Mezzanine over to Stationery. I
remember Alam always called Stephanie,

> "*Stevanie,*"
> or just,
> "*Steve.*"

I think I even vaguely recall Stephanie meeting
Keith and telling me that he was teaching her to
eat fire and that it was incredible; this while we
were having seltzer water and Little Debbies in
the Afghani luncheonette below my then—
Manhattan apartment. And then one day at least
a few years after that, because Stephanie had very
long hair, I ran into her on the Williamsburg Bridge,
and she told me about Bindlestiff, and that they
were making their living entirely on it. That was
in the mid-90s, and they have been ever since.

So I was eagerly anticipating the Cirkus.

> Liz had mentioned that if you came to
> the show dressed as a clown you could
> get in for free, or for three dollars, I don't
> remember, but it was appealing to me.

This would have been when I was making a living

as a freelance shelver at the bookstore; the success of this lifestyle was contingent on keeping a tight budget, to say the least.

I was dressing up a lot in those days, mostly for Rocky Horror but also for my literary readings; I was comfortable experimenting with makeup and loved excuses to go out in costume. But I ran into the problem that I really couldn't picture a good clown face and didn't have any books illustrating one. The thing with pancake makeup is that it is not subtle. You really have to come up with a design and commit to it. And once you've done something dramatic it can really transform the look of your face, and even how you feel; what is drawn out of you. It's why I liked doing readings in costume: I could feel the transformation from neurotic book clerk to confident female creature, at least for a time.

I landed on a harlequin clown image in my head, maybe from Picasso's Blue Period. Diamonds over my eyes—just keep it simple, I thought. Sometimes less is more when it comes to covering your whole face in stage makeup. The result, though, came out looking far more like the fifth member of KISS. And immediately after seeing my face in the mirror in this persona, I got a raging headache. I sat around my apartment for a while like this, wondering about what to do. Worrying about what my friend would have to resort to if I didn't show up at the Cirkus. Worrying that even if she reached me on the phone, she'd never find me way out in the sticks of Greenpoint by herself. This was in 2000, when Greenpoint seemed like a relative wilderness and still well before everyone in New York had a cell phone.

Well, I finally had to admit that I was too ill to do anything, that Ace Frehley had stolen my evening and my good health, and I took that damn makeup off. I never heard from Liz until the next day. She said she got to the show late, went in and yelled my whole name at the top of her lungs a few times, and got it that I wasn't there. Then she ran into some other friends and crashed with them.

It was years later, when I called a whole different city home, that I had the pleasure of watching "*Stevanie*" eat fire.

Russ Josephs
I WAS A SCIENTOLOGIST!

My first job after college was as a film critic for a Portland, Oregon paper called The Papeback Jukebox, an "alternative weekly" that most people just read for the listings. The pay sucked, but I got to see a crapload of films for free.

After a while, I grew bored, and I wanted to write actual stories, to dig up some dirt, to do some real reporting. I asked Julie, the editor, if this would be okay, and she said fine, as long as she liked the idea. The next day I had it, she loved it, and I eagerly began preparing for my new undercover adventure. Following in the footsteps of Hollywood's finest– John Travolta, Tom Cruise, Juliette Lewis–I was going to be a Scientologist.

I was equally fascinated and freaked-out by them, and always wondered what went on in their centers, a number of which dotted the downtown landscape. So one afternoon I walked into their main building, which had a large sign outside that read: "Free personality test. Inquire within." A man met me in the lobby, and I told him that I was interested in pursuing my spiritual development, and that his organization seemed like the right place to begin. He greeted me warmly, telling me that I was indeed correct, that he could help me, and led me to a room with a copy of the test. He offered me some coffee, which I politely refused, having watched too many documentaries on cults–the Moonies, the Branch Davidians–and was worried that it was laced.

The test was extremely long, filled with ridiculously general questions many that seemed to overlap:

> *"Have you ever felt depressed? Do you sometimes make remarks you later regret? Are you prejudiced against your own school or team?"*

Some were just plain stupid: *"Does emotional music have an effect on you? Do you bite your fingernails?"*

The thing was obviously designed to play to one's insecurities, to make the person taking it appear like they were beyond reproach, and how lucky they were to have taken it under the auspices of Scientology, where they could be saved! I answered the questions as truthfully as I could, and when I finished it I handed it to the man, who immediately processed it.

Upon viewing the results, I was planning to act suitably disaffected and in dire need of help so they would take me seriously, but I hardly needed to. What should have been a rising and falling graph depicting my emotional status, was instead a straight line that ran across the bottom of the page, underneath the mark that said: "Normal." It made me out to be depressed, paranoid, anxious and suicidal. The guy watched as I looked at the results and then stared deep into my eyes.

"It looks like you've come to the right place."

He then introduced me to one of his associates, a very pleasant and upbeat woman who took me into another room, a copy of the results before her. She echoed the man's sentiments, and said that I had chosen wisely to seek help from them, as it looked like I really needed it. I played right into this, and told her that since college I'd felt alienated and alone, was prone to mood swings, and was at a loss at to how to proceed. She said that scores of others before me had been helped, and all I had to do was to sign up for an introductory course, which started at seventy-five dollars.

"But you guys are a religion, right?" I said. *"Like a church or something?"*

"Yes, that's correct."

"Well, going to church doesn't normally cost anything."

"You still have to give to the collection plate."

"True, but that's like what? A dollar? I'm sorry, but I can't afford the class."

"But I really think you should take it," she said, smiling and opening her eyes wide, wide, wide. *"Think about it this way: what's money compared to spiritual happiness? A small investment now is nothing compared to the future riches you'll acquire with greater self-esteem and strength."*

"But I don't have the seventy-five dollars."

"Couldn't you save up if you wanted to?" she asked, her smile fading. *"It's really not that much when you think about it."*

"Isn't there any other way? Could I work it off? Sweep the floors or something?"

"No, I'm afraid we don't do that."

This sucked. I needed more information to write the story, so I asked her if she wouldn't mind telling me a little bit about the organization, what they were all about, I'd learn if I did take the class. To this she gave me a vague explanation about how their founder L. Ron traveled extensively with his grandfather who was in the navy (do they allow small children on naval vessels?), and what he witnessed all over the world greatly disturbed him: everywhere, people were unhappy. Also, people were struggling to survive (he was fucking astute). He decided he wanted to find a way to make people's lives better, and used his science fiction books to finance extensive psychological research (a small investment for future riches?). Thus, Dianetics, and eventually Scientology, was born.

She went on to describe the basic philosophy. According to Hubbard's research, the brain was divided into two parts, the active mind (conscious) and the reactive mind (subconscious). The former housed all productivity, artistry and positive thought. Everything that held someone down, whether it be fear, insecurity or painful memories, was located in the latter. To bridge this gap, his program worked to completely eliminate the reactive mind. The successful candidate was then "clear," and able to live a healthy, productive, unobstructed life. I didn't really get this, and didn't think it made much sense, let alone jived with my own personal philosophy. I was all about the unconscious.

"What about dreams?" I asked her.
   "They stem completely from the subconscious. Do you guys stop having them or something?"
"We don't really deal with dreams," she said, growing annoyed with my questions.

She handed me a brochure of the various classes they offered, and told me again that I should really think about taking the introductory class. Then she stood up and said she had something else to take care of, and led me to the exit.

I left extremely disappointed, my Scientology career over before it had begun. I practically had nothing to write about, so I resorted to an exaggerated, tongue-in-cheek rendering of my experience. I described how I was never left alone like in a real cult, how the people I met had twinkling, other-worldly eyes like Charles Manson, how I was expecting at any second to be kidnapped and brainwashed, where I would ultimately have to be saved and deprogrammed. I also included a copy of my personality test with the flatline at the bottom. Because I had heard horror stories about acts of retaliation from the group, I wrote the piece under the alias L. Russ Hubbel.

When the issue came out, there wasn't much local reaction, except for mild amusement, and I was sure that my fears had been unwarranted. Then, a few days later, we started getting reports from people that they couldn't find the paper anywhere, that none of the stores or kiosks that usually carried it had any in stock. We always printed off more copies than were necessary, and this had never happened before, so my first reaction was that the story was so good that people were nabbing them left and right. But the truth was that the Scientologists had gotten wind of it, and snatched up every issue they could find.

Soon we began receiving a series of threatening phone calls from them. At first, they simply declaimed the piece, forcefully requesting to speak to me, wanting to know my home number, my address. When they realized that this was not going to happen, they started calling back repeatedly, just to tie up the phone lines. They did this for weeks, apparently having operatives working around the clock with nothing to do sans dial and re-dial our number.

Then it got worse. They began showing up at our office, several of them at a time, demanding to speak to me. What they wanted I had no idea, but they were so aggressive and ill-tempered I didn't want to find out. Following Lisa's advice, I stayed away from the place, and didn't even leave my apartment, for fear I'd somehow be recognized and attacked, kidnapped, killed. I became a virtual hermit, only venturing outside to go the supermarket, and even then I'd wear a hat and sunglasses. I was scared to death, although, truth be told, it was pretty exciting. My first real piece and people wanted to kill me. But, just to be on the safe side, after that I went back to the film reviews.

Soon we began receiving a series of threatening phone calls from them. At first, they simply declaimed the piece, forcefully requesting to speak to me, wanting to know my home number, my address. When they realized that this was not going to happen, they started calling back repeatedly, just to tie up the phone lines. They did this for weeks, apparently having operatives working around the clock with nothing to do sans dial and re–dial our number.

Then it got worse. They began showing up at our office, several of them at a time, demanding to speak to me. What they wanted I had no idea, but they were so aggressive and ill-tempered I didn't want to find out. Following Lisa's advice, I stayed away from the place, and didn't even leave my apartment, for fear I'd somehow be recognized and attacked, kidnapped, killed. I became a virtual hermit, only venturing outside to go the supermarket, and even then I'd wear a hat and sunglasses. I was scared to death, although, truth be told, it was pretty exciting. My first real piece and people wanted to kill me. But, just to be on the safe side, after that I went back to the film reviews.

Tiffany Stevens
MR. BIG

Let's
start
at
the end.
The other woman showed up. I knew it was coming. That despite what he and I had, it was explicitly temporary and she was the one he was really waiting for. I simply had been biding his time. And as usual, it's the ending that's vivid and that gets replayed in the moments when I come home expecting to see him only to find my empty apartment But she was his real owner.

Mr. Big is a black and white tuxedo cat I cat sat at my apartment from Sunday to Sunday one wet cold week in November. His owner, my friend Kendall, a fellow Texan is the kind of sassy Texan I wish I were. She had named Mr. Big when she was single and he walked into her door as a stray at the height of Sex and the City zeitgeist.

I'm the single one now, dipping my toe in my thirties and, egads, getting divorced. I've never had a cat before, never spent more than an hour or two with one. But I've often thought about the idea of it. And I do think they're cute.

Between manic jogging to exhaust myself, moving to a random part of Brooklyn to escape vivid city memories, and being recommended Eat, Pray, Love (I still can't bring myself to read it) every five minutes this year of life has been busy ripping through my guts and the world no longer makes much sense. I sometimes forget how to breathe and despite changing my hair color and obsessively reading my horoscope, I have no idea who I am and what's going to happen next. Life is weird outside the cadence of my old (young) life. We met freshman year of college and that was that, it was buzzy bliss and then we just went blank together after our respective 30th birthdays, a little over a year ago.

I've attempted to fill the crater in my life in various healthy and unhealthy ways, then decided to ignore it, which of course, caused me to fall right into it completely. I've been down here by myself for awhile, so anyway, cue the cat.

Kendall was off for the holiday. This all started with a breezy phone call during which was sprinkled in:

"Hey, would you mind checking in on Mr. Big over the Thanksgiving weekend? He's really easy, he's a doll"

"Sure, of course. No problem."

A few minutes later we were setting up a time for her to drop him off at my house for seven days.

In between grief and distraction, I've crafted both longwinded narrative explanations and scripted elaborate confrontations I know will never happen to make sense of the break. So many words, so little understanding. Mostly it's his fault. For not loving me enough, and in not the exact right way. Kendall showed up with the cat, cat crate and accessories. She ran down the basics while Mr. Big pattered around his new digs.

"Anything else I need to know? Should I change anything around here, could he hurt himself?" I asked.

"Nah, have fun. Whatever, he's good, he mostly sleeps, no worries. Thanks so much."

"Oh, it's….."

"Mr. Big! Ha har. Look at him, only here two minutes and already he's thinks its his house. Licking his balls. Typical man!

Ha! Thanks again, honey."

"Oh, well, wow, of course of course. Sure. Have a great trip."

Mr. Big moved in and I turned a few of my scarce kitchen supplies into food and water bowls for him and made a bed on the floor with kitchen towels. Why haven't I gotten around to buying actual plates and flatware and pots and pans? Why have I kept my house so inhospitable? I cleaned up the living room, it seemed kind of unseemly, the way I was living. Duly spiffed up I attempted to play with Mr. Big, tossing the ball around. He approached me. Now is the part where I mention than not only am I allergic to cats I am also kind of afraid of them. All the scratching and shrieking. That kind of unpredictability is unnerving. I hesitated and touched his head, stroking him gently and saying his name, he accepted this and I felt mild relief. I then left the house for longer than I usually would.

Immediately on my return I deluged him with catnip, and he became a junkie running into the walls and licking stray nip off of the floor. Then just laying in odd positions and staring into space. How embarrassing. I had that phase myself about six months ago.

As I mindlessly Interneted a few minutes later, he entered the room. He went to the closet, with the full length mirror on the outside of the door. He looked at this new cat and started pawing at it. *"Who is this that cat I'm encountering,"* he seemed puzzled and spent minutes and minutes pawing the mirror trying to figure it out. I had that phase too. I canceled my MySpace account and never got a Facebook one.

It was my turn. He approached me and starting meowing, I asked him what he wanted. He didn't answer. I thought cats were supposed to be easy. I was compulsively reading my horoscope and did not want to be bothered, it felt annoying to get up and check his water, litter box and food, all fine. I sat down and gave him an accusing stare, then turned back to the computer. This is why I live alone. And I like it, I can't have all these demands on me. He meowed and pawed the chair leg. I typed. He pawed my leg, this time with his claws out. Oh, God, he's going to kill me. I summoned my courage

"Mr. Big. That's it! Get out of here, go lay on your bed."

I threw his toy ball out of the room. He didn't budge. He pierced though me with his eyes. I cleared my throat. He settled at my feet. Close call.

Minutes pass, I got distracted and relaxed. He saw his chance and lunged up at me. I was frozen. He landed on my lap, did an exploratory leg cat paw massage and curled up purring. Time stopped and I felt his fat little warm furry body against my legs and stomach. I realized this was the first prolonged contact I've had with another living being in the calendar year 2007. I put my hand on his back and hot tears streamed down my face.

"Okay, okay. Sleep, Mr. Big. Sleep."

I had to answer the phone and go to the bathroom and I was hungry. But I sat there reading the page already on the screen until he woke up, moving only to wet the sleeve of my hoodie on my face and pet him.

I was feeling edgy by nightfall and went for a manic run, my head filled with drama, my ears with music, pounding the Prospect Park loop and my own body into tiredness. As I opened the front door, Mr. Big stood there until I bonded with him by throwing his ball around. It was fun to have someone to come home to again.

But as I took care of things around the apartment and got ready to get into the shower, he kept getting under my feet. I needed a break. He started shriek meowing and showing fang. He blocked me in the hall. I went around him. I locked the bathroom door and took a really long shower. He was waiting at the bathroom door when I emerged fang meowing and rubbing against my wetish legs, depositing cat hair over all of my cleanness.

"Aaarrgghhh. You do this just to annoy me, Mr. Big. Just leave me alone."

He meowed in agreement, then lost interest and went to another room. I had forgotten to empty his litter box and had to go to the cold outside trash with wet hair.

I went to bed, wondering what he was going to do. After the lap nap of the afternoon, I was hoping he would sleep near me. Oh God, I am becoming one of Those Women. Forget it, I corrected my own thoughts. I do not want that. Forget it.

I woke up, or rather was woken up at I don't know how early. I shoved him (gently) away eight different times, it was almost enough to actually wake me up. A few hours later I did wake up rested. I was lying flat, he had been asleep over the covers in the crook of my legs. He roused and approached. I was defenseless, what would he do?

"Okay, okay. Come here"

I mimicked control of the situation and made a place for him next to me. He came about ten inches closer than I intended and curled up in the curve of my neck and purred. We both fell back asleep. Rousing again he leaned in. I held my breath. He sniffed around. I closed my eyes, preparing for the worst. He began dutifully licking my face. I couldn't stop giggling. His little pink tongue was sandpapery.

Every day after school in college and grad school, the boy who became a man and then became my husband and I would lay on the bed and go over our respective anecdotes, attempting to outdo each other with funny stories and impersonations of people we had encountered during the day. These sessions almost always ended in a warm quiet with messy hair and tickling and a type of mutualness I often wonder if I will ever feel again. So much understanding, and no words.

The next day at the computer I was typing and Mr. Big came into the room, bored with his scratching post. After he had some of his mirror pawing I was ready for my lap time and summoned him over. I tired again and again to get him to come to me. At first saying his name, then by tricking him with playing, then by overenthusiastically patting my lap and trying and trying to get his attention and waiting. He wasn't interested... He took a nap on the bed instead. I felt pangs of disappointment. I decided it was crazy and I didn't care. I was glad he would be gone in a few days.

Constantly thinking about his food and water, playing enough, finding the toys he kept hiding, making sure it was impossible for him to hurt himself, making sure he didn't get out of my apartment when the door was open, and chasing him back to the apartment if he did, it was more intense than I reckoned. I had to be more consistent and mindful than I have been in awhile.

Sunday came, I woke up in the morning and our now familiar routine of morning purring and face licking. Usually, I sit up a bit and pet him and he curls up to me. But on his last day I was especially tired and relaxed and stayed flat, not even lifting my head. He came and sat up this time. First giving me the cat paw massage on my shoulder and sniffing around and then licking my face to make sure everything was in order. As I laid flat, he surveyed the room, stayed alert and looked around. I dozed off, feeling more relaxed than I have since I can remember, my face rolling right into his paws. He put his paw protectively over my hand and stayed up keeping an eye on things as I slept and I was still under safe watch when I woke up.

I came home from my morning jog on Monday and put my leg in the empty space of the opening door to block him from getting out, a phantom defense, I had forgotten my time with him was over. I had the place all to myself now

He was gone.

Jaime Borschuk
PLEASE DON'T CONFRONT ME
WITH MY FAILURES

Today I randomly and separately saw 3 people with whom I've had poor romantic relationships. After the first two, I came home and buried my face in my pillow, thinking there must be some kind of meaningful punishment in such visual deliverance. But then I thought, no, I had been having a great weekend in which I was delighting myself with all kinds of positive thoughts. These visions were just showing me the difference, right? So I moved on with my evening, and went out forbeers with a friend. I was in line to pee at Zeigeist when I saw dud #3. When he realized it was me,my turn was up and he followed me into the bathroom, closed the door behind us and abruptly began extracting blow from a vial. Hmph.

>*"How are you doing?" I asked.*

>*"Not so good."*

>*"Oh?"*

>*"Yeah, I'm seeing this 22 year old girl…"*
He said while taking a snort.

I caught a glimpse of post-nasal drip. He looked at the vial, then at me, and his eyes politely told me that he wished he had more to offer.

>*"Huh, yeah, didn't you break things off with me?"*
I asked myself in disbelief, apparently out loud.

>*"No, you don't understand, I was doing you a favor. I'm a bad person."*

And I realized he was right. About the favor. Despite his relentlessly altered perspective, he was still able to sense that I wasn't like him and that I have the capacity to draw more satisfying attention. Maybe he's not such a bad person. I felt oddly thankful and, after I finished peeing and he fastened his blow vial shut, we stepped back into the bar and parted ways.

On Saturday I had coffee with a new friend who said that he found it really hard to date in San Francisco because people are frequently in transition and fairly determined to keep all of their options open. He also said that he liked mid-westerners because they return phone calls, make plans and follow through. I said Amen to that, wishing that my Iowa roots would take a slightly firmer grip. Could these Iowa roots be my chaperone?

A few nights ago I had a dream about a blue lemon. It was a really smooth and shiny blue lemon, with dimples. In the dream, I showed it to my dad. In real life, I want to paint it, because it had such a strong appearance in the dream that I can't really explain it in words. It reminded me of the blue that Rebecca Solnit describes. The blue on the horizon that is the light that never reaches us. I started to think that the blue lemon was perhaps a sign for all the things I was never meant to be. The failures I thought were supposed to be successes. I thought of the blue lemon tonight while staring at the baby blue porcelain sink in the bathroom at Bolompie, and wondered if I could just wash my hands of my old approaches.

Eric Nelson
YOUNG, DUMB AND FULL OF INK

At parties, especially in the summer, at least one person will ask me about the prominent tattoo on my neck and where it came from. This is what I tell them—

The conversation on the pay phone on a street somewhere in Budapest went something like this:

"Honey, I'm bringing you back a few special souvenirs. And I'm bad at keeping surprises… I got your name tattooed on my neck!"

"Oh my God! Really?"

"Yeah, I can't wait to get home and show you!"

It was true. In script writing, on the lower right side of my neck was "Allison." At some point in a two week, self-financed backpacking trip through Europe six years ago I made the decision to get my girlfriend's name permanently marked on my body in a prominent place. Of course I made sure a tie could cover it, but I knew I'd show it more than the others. I had enough tattoos already and most importantly I would surely marry her.

The shop was on a side street in Prague. A man who's English was limited to *"Oh, New York! Hardcore! Old-school tattoo!"* did a wonderful job for ultimately a cheap price in a sanitary setting. I was dumb, but not THAT dumb. Of course everyone except my future ex-fiancé and I disagreed.

The predictable happened: both the marriage and my thug ex-wifey's name neck tattoo weren't meant to be.

Three years later I sat in a tattoo shop in Paterson, New Jersey, getting inked by a friend of a coworker. We stepped outside the shop for a cigarette break in the setting sun; I glad to see my car still there. This time the conversation went like this:

"Shit, we shoulda taken a 'before' picture before we started," said the artist.

"Well, you can probably still do it," I replied.

"When we get back in we'll take some photos. You won't ever DO THAT again, eh?"

"No....no, I won't."

Of course, logic tells you that the silhouette of a city skyscape and "Your Name" is bigger in size than simply "Allison." And it is. I decided on that based on the fact that I knew I'd be living in a city for an extended period of time. Of course, the latter half is a joke, albeit a joke I had spoken of wanting to stamp on my ass for years beforehand.

Nowadays when I tell the story, I laugh. And it's genuine. One morning you look in the bathroom mirror, smile and blush. Another you sob and think of quietly hanging yourself. Another, you smile, shake your head and close your eyes.

And finally, you laugh. You laugh at the naivety of it, and how ridiculous the final product is. You laugh because even though you still make dumb decisions that is one you won't repeat. You laugh the loudest while telling the story to other people because it actually happened to you.

Josh Medsker
MY NAME

I went through a phase, as I'm sure many kids have, when I was disgusted by my name. Josh. Josh. I'd repeat to myself just to make sure it was as bad as I thought it was. Sixth grade was when it started. I was five ten, and a hundred pounds. I was shy, awkward, you get the picture. There was a swirlie with my name on it, waiting for me when I hit junior high.

My name just had this thing about it—this *"sh"* on the end of it that seemed to lull people to sleep. JoSHHHH. It was just so goddamned wussy. I mean, it just sort of faded out you know? My name said, *"Be quiet!"* My name did not command respect. By god, I was going to change it.

Now, I knew that Joshua was a legendary Jewish leader who fought the battle of Jericho, and knocked down the walls and yadda yadda yadda, but I was not that guy. I was a twelve year old beanpole with shaggy white hair, saddled with a bad name.

I briefly considered using my middle name, Anthony. I was named after one of my Dad's Vietnam War buddies. War did sound pretty manly... but Tony Medsker didn't sound quite right.

Plus, I really liked my initials. J.A.M. In fact, I liked them so much I made sort of a logo out of it. I drew it on everything. That's the kind of nerd I was. It was like my personal stamp. I might as well have hung a big sign around my neck that said, "*I'm a dork! Please publicly humiliate me!*"

I thought maybe I could change my name to Jack, or John. Good hearty, macho names like that. Johnny Medsker almost sounded like boxer, or a baseball player. And I was already an ace outfielder in Little League, so how perfect was that? I could just hear them—"*Hey Johnny! Throw that grounder in here, kid!*"

Still, everyone at my school knew me as Josh. Josh Mudsucker. Osh Kosh B' Josh. But it was still six years before I turned eighteen and could legally change my name, or move away.

Tony. Tony Medsker. No way. I was screwed.

DIGITAL ROT

CHRIS REALLY LIKES DOUBLE DRAGON.

DO YOU KNOW IT? IT'S AN ARCADE GAME FROM 1987.

X-BOX 360, THE VIDEO GAME SYSTEM, DOES A THING WHERE PLAYERS CAN DOWNLOAD A GAME FOR A FEE.

INSTEAD OF BUYING A HARD COPY OF A GAME AT A STORE, YOU BUY IT ONLINE AND HAVE IT STORED ON THE SYSTEM'S HARD DRIVE.

THAT'S WHAT CHRIS D[ID] WITH DOUBLE DRAGO[N].

This is the p[art] where you c[an] knock Abobo down the pi[t]

BUT THEN, THE GAME SIMPLY STOPPED WORKING ONE DAY. CHRIS TRIED TO RE-DOWNLOAD IT; TO NO AVAIL.

WHAT THEEE FFF—

IT TURNS OUT THE COMPA[NY] THAT PORTED IT TO THE 360 WENT OUT OF BUSIN[ESS]

Spent 10 bucks on a game I can't even play anymore.

Betsy Housten
MOTEL SHOW

That was the last night of the Bridge Motel. We were leafing through that week's issue of the Stranger when we saw the story. The motel, with its crumbling pink paint, incriminating address on the edge of town, and close proximity to the city's most popular suicide jump the Aurora Bridge, had long endured a damning reputation as emblematic of Seattle's seedy underbelly. It was legendary, preserved in the collective memory of the municipality the way people talk about 42nd Street in the eighties or Amsterdam's Red Light District. There had been murders here, said the papers, traveling salesmen and prostitutes, needles in the sheets and crack pipes under the beds. The cops had all but given up on the place, which had recently been condemned for demolition by local authorities. The only reasonably good fortune to befall its sagging structure in years had occurred when the building's latest manager recognized the inherent potential of such a history and turned the motel over to a bunch of performance artists to give it a proper goodbye. And so, for one night in rainy September, it would welcome dozens of guests—free of charge—to peer into its grimy walls and behold the spectacles within.

Andy and I weren't the only ones who found the idea irresistible. Kids from all over the city poured in, down Route 99 and around the hairpin bend just preceding the parking lot. Some people welcomed the imminent removal of what they considered a dilapidated eyesore; others lamented its passing as cultural landmark, this gateway to a wilder dimension, this last stop for the desperate. The hallways, the balconies, the lobby, and of course the rooms themselves all spoke of nights long gone, illicit and hidden away from the world. To step inside was to find yourself immediately curious about the countless reasons someone would rent a bedroom for just one night–the lingering feelings of the people who had taken up within its walls, where they had come from and the things they'd done while they'd been here. What they'd been thinking; the why, and the how, and the inevitable what now.

Tonight, there was a room bathed in pink light, ankle-high with salt and strewn with torn-up letters. We left our shoes at the door and picked through the pieces, reading whatever we found, sometimes aloud, knowing none of it would really add up to anything. Another room contained a portable radio that broadcasted scratchy music over a single lit lamp and an eerily empty bed. Several conspicuously placed objects reclined on the few available surfaces – a man's glove, a lace blanket, a teddy bear, things that didn't really belong in hired rooms and were somehow frightening in their arrogant, unexplained innocence. Still another room featured a human-sized box of fluorescent twine hung at crazy angles from the walls and ceiling, crookedly stretching to graze the heads and elbows of anyone who opened the door and, realizing it had shut behind them, had to crawl through it.

Crowds hung in the parking lot, drinking beer and rustling paper plates, glancing casually around in an effort to appear like they'd only shown up because everyone else had. I wondered which of them had been here before, or if, like us, this was their first visit. Andy and I wandered around hand in hand, mostly silent; every once in awhile one of us would sigh, or point, or offer up an appreciative glance. I loved her so much right then.

We walked past a series of scrambled black–and–white images projected onto a second-floor wall, depicting events that seemed significant if for no other reason than they were here, with the others. Suddenly something deep in my stomach pulled itself taut and rung out as if it had been struck. It echoed throughout my body, long and low and exquisitely mournful.

Back on the ground floor a young girl served small plastic cups of red wine in a makeshift box office, all black cardboard and velvet curtains. A hand–lettered sign next to her elbow read "SPIRITS: ONE DOLLAR"; her face alternated between a smile and a scowl. Behind her, someone had relieved room 103 of its furniture, where a woman and a man now stalked back and forth, smearing ketchup on their faces and tweed clothing, as well as the peeling wallpaper from which glowered streaky bulls-eyes and random sequences of numbers. We threaded through the hushed assemblage and found a couple of spots to sit, right up front. Andy settled into my lap; I wrapped my arms around her belly and rested my chin on her left shoulder. On the bile-green carpet under the performers' feet drifted Styrofoam plates and bits of drainpipe, frayed segments of twine and upended aluminum cans. They wore no shoes. Their dialogue was weird and irreverent and ominous, and it looped if you stayed long enough, which we did.

Any other day I would probably have dismissed it as pretentiously obscure, the brainchild of bored actors with an unwieldy reliance on shock value for its own sake. I definitely wouldn't have driven out of my way for it on a Friday night. But I couldn't move; I was captivated. Maybe it was the three thousand miles that stretched between the Bridge Motel and Brooklyn, maybe it was the palpable tragedy of our long-distance love affair, and maybe it was that something in the Pacific Northwest air that made everything feels simultaneously calmer and more alive. The man paced faster, tightening his obsessive circles. The woman held a huge knife in the air and growled—at him, at us, at herself. I wanted it never to stop, wanted to sit in this spot exactly forever, and I knew without speaking that Andy felt the same.

When her friends pushed through the crowd and beckoned to us, I thought we could just pretend not to see them. They, for their part, had had enough, seen their fill of the disturbing reminders of human depravities past, and wanted out–wanted to go back to their lives, have a drink, maybe take a shower and laugh about how creepy the whole thing was. Remember that night, they'd say later, those freaky people and that nasty old motel. They squirmed in the face of the grotesque and stepped carefully out of its reach; this was the crucial distinction. Andy and I knew that beyond this waited a world much less interesting–one littered with too-short visits and too-tired phone calls, a slippery tower of escalating misunderstandings and the restless, growing dread that we were just too different. We were best when we could see a crazy thing happen right in front of us, could point and say There, that's what's really fucked up, all this little stuff doesn't matter, just hang onto me and we'll be all right. And just as soon as I realized this, I knew it was over. Her weight in my lap grew heavier. Our ride was still standing in the wings, gesturing more impatiently with every passing moment. And we had no other way to get home. So slowly we stood, making an elaborate show of stretching our limbs and brushing off our clothes, in one last attempt to convince them it was wrong to leave.

Cecelia Mariscal
SUBMISSION

I'm trapped in an airplane surrounded by screaming children trying to remember when my hands were tiny and resembled tissue paper cutouts. Haven't these people heard of benadryl? I try to think and summon my Mother or my cousin to give me patience so that I can go six hours without making a smart-ass comment designed to hurt feelings but they are where I am going and not where I am. I want to order beer indefinitely as if this airplane ride were my destination and not San Diego itself. The ride is all I care about. As long as I am moving I'm spared the sanctity of the moment. I do not have to feel you, pay attention to you or consider your needs. I can just live on a vibration. Never seen and only temporarily felt.

I don't know why I come back year after year. We love each other cause there is no choice and not cause we grew to do it. How do you choose and not choose to love somebody. It must be because it does not exist. Who are all these idiots waiting for this religious experience but me and my family

...we got the same blood. It pumps and it runs like the Rio Grande carryin' every Mexican back home. Apparently that's all we need.

I feebly raise my hand. Yea, that's me.

Three and half hours to go. You'd think I'd savor it but I pound the minutes into my eyes until they disappear. I'm way ahead of the speed of light now. I'm already forty with children grown. Tiny hands with bones that shot out like branches complete with briefcases, porches, dogs and car seats. They get taller and I shrivel and become dry. Divorced or never married. My head pounds as the minutes get deeper and expand and grow and become fat like hours, years...decades. I am the savviest traveler you'll ever meet. I want some kind of medal for it. I want something to show for it. I have no stories or scenes in my memory. I just have the airplane and this ticking in my head.

LAUREN NICOLE NIXON

I. I ate a grapefruit and left the peel on the windowsill, let the sun kiss it for a few days. I watched it rot and harden, a circus of flies crowding the bitter rind. I watched em buzz for an hour or so, then walked away from the mess. If mother were to see the flies, the larvae, hatching, new lives blooming, she'd have a fit. But mama, I'm telling you, I like the filth of things.

II. Choose a loaf of bread (sourdough, white, honey wheat, pumpernickel). Something sturdy and seeable. Begin at the barn, tearing and dropping hunks of bread from the barn to your new destination. You will know when you've found a good place to stop cause your shoulders will feel like feathers and your insides'll glimmer and blink like Orion. If you must go back, just follow the trail of crumbs. But just so you know, the barn has just burned down.

In the Break or Wading

There is something
desirable about
breaking your
mama's china or

testing the durability
of a family heirloom.

First the grip of it
in your hands, the planned
slippage of your fingers
then

crash, splatter, wham
your ankles are sliced
up in your own mess.

You are wading in
something that's briny

and pleasant all at once.

and there is comfort in
breaking in new sheets
with several lovers.

the wrinkle, the purring
linen, a boudoir

sounding so much better

than a bedroom, sounding
so much better than
sainthood.

You are waist-deep
in some ocean

without a map, a compass/

with mud between your
thighs .

You are rumpling/
folding/then rumpling
again.

Gus Iversen
DIFFERENT DIRECTIONS

There were two Indian women on the subway. Each of them wearing a colorful sari and holding an enormous blue cart at their feet. Like a grocery cart but twice as big. The carts were filled with large cloth sacks, which were filled with I don't know what. The older one had a small stud in her nose. We were sitting directly across from each other and I wondered if they had just arrived from India or maybe Bangladesh. I looked closely at their mouths and tried to see if they were the kind of mouths that form English words.

A man with a gray goatee and a Puerto Rico baseball cap sat down next to the older one and accidentally brushed her elbow. They smiled at each other in the way people on the subway do when unintentional contact has been made. She then turned away from him and back towards me. She put her head on her daughter's shoulder and giggled uncontrollably. Her eyes had fireworks in them. I imagined he was the first American she had exchanged idle pleasantries with. Between bouts of laughter she would whisper a strange language in her daughters ear. My heart nearly exploded, I diverted my eyes and concentrated on those mysterious cloth sacks. I wanted to know their secrets.

In Berlin I met a Russian man at 4 o'clock in the morning. We were the only people around and we both wanted company. I spoke zero Russian and he spoke zero English. We drank two beers together, throwing non-sequitors back and forth to the keep the silence at bay. His countenance was sort of frightening but I decided it was just a cultural thing. I imagine our conversation may have gone something like this.

"I am going to Prague in two hours. Sad to leave Berlin. Beautiful people here."

"I don't understand a word you just said. What a shitty night it's been!"

"Umm… yea. Ah. Have you ever been there? I want to see the Charles Bridge."

"You're a strange person, aren't you? Thank god for beer. Why on Earth haven't you gone home yet?"

"…My sister broke her leg once taking out the garbage…"

One morning in Amsterdam I awoke to find a ladybug had made a home for herself in my belly button. I had been dreaming about flowers. Beautiful flowers of all different colors and impossible compositions. They were everywhere and for some reason I lacked coordination and kept stepping in their beds. Every time I stepped on a different flower it made me feel terrible. I really didn't want to step on them, but my muscles were not in my control. So to awake from this dream and find a ladybug had made a home out of my belly button – well, I stayed in bed extra long so as not to disturb it.

When I finally got up I scooped my little tenant onto my finger and she walked around a little bit.

She was disoriented with sleep but at least I hadn't squashed her. I hopped down from my bunk bed and took her to the porch. This woke up my Italian roommates. I told them all about it but I'm not sure it really came across. I do not speak Italian.

It was the first time I'd been out of The United States in over fifteen years. I was traveling alone and I only got back a week ago. Ever since returning home people have been talking to me more on the streets. They ask me for directions, they comment about how nice the weather is, one little kid even asked me to pet his dog. Nobody spoke to me before the trip. I had been closed off somehow without knowing it. Furthermore, certain elements of the tourist still compel me; the landscape will not be lost on my lens. This is New York City, after all.

The Indian women, they understood this. It was an enthusiasm we shared. They got off the train at 104th St., deep in Queens. Their gargantuan carts thumping as they jostled from the train to the platform. They pushed their carts westward, the mother walking ahead of the daughter. I continued on until 121st St. in Kew Gardens. I don't live here. I am cat sitting here for a friend of a friend while she is in Seoul negotiating fabrics. That was a long train ride. I was on my way back from downtown Manhattan. You can sit on the steps of Federal Hall with its bricks and winding sidewalks and forget for a moment that this is where you live.

Aditi Sriram
TAKING DIRECTIONS FROM A SUNSET

The energy pulses from the crescent-shaped streetlamps and rustles in the palm trees. It slaps you in the face along with the heat, as you step off the plane and take in your first breaths of Egyptian air. Inside the airport, restless tour guides take over with a swagger you come to identify in every Egyptian man. They bark in Arabic to their colleagues and brandish popsong–singing cell phones. Conversation, commotion and smoke arc across the ceilings, buzzing indiscriminately in everybody's ears.

You become keenly aware of men everywhere. Bushy eyebrows, abundant facial hair, tall figures, Cleopatran noses, handsome faces, wide grins greet each other with kisses, hugs, cigarettes and praise to God;
Al Hamdullilah!

"Welcome in Cairo," a sign reads.

First stop, the Nile. The 'Corniche' is the name given to the street on either side of the banks of the epic river. You walk along the shaded street, ducking under palm tree leaves eager to bid you salaam and stepping over stray cats, and you get a sense that there's more to this river.

The rich voice of the muezzin, who performs the call to God five times a day from the mosque, penetrates the air. You expect a Cinderella effect–people turning into prostrating pumpkins–but no such metamorphosis occurs. Idleness hangs like a heavy curtain in the polluted air of Cairo that vehicles and people struggle through at every moment. Cars crawl because of the hordes of pedestrians threading carelessly through them. Men wield their lust like their cigarettes–unhealthily, frequently and carelessly. They call out to you, a look, a leer, a word, a verb, a full sentence bludgeoning your comfort and dignity, and you wish there was a real curtain hanging from the sky that you could hide behind. You admire the nonplussed local women who tuck their phones into their head–wrapping hijab, making them Bluetooth friendly, while men tuck their machismo into their pants; it oozes out uselessly.

That evening you visit Al-Azhar mosque. You pad through the heavy gate, barefoot, and encounter utter peace. In spite of the bustle raging on the street just steps away, a gentle hush has settled over the huge courtyard–blowing away the heavy curtain from earlier–and you can't help but whisper. Domes bulge, then taper into a perfect point, their curves both calming and alluring. You are struck by the detail everywhere, everywhere. Lattice work on the doors, patterns painted on the ceilings, calligraphy etched onto the walls, lights casting the enormous structure in a divine glow. You sit on the soft carpet and your head naturally tilts back to gaze upon the towers sprouting from every corner. You're moved to pray, to ponder, to stop thinking and allow the mosque to work its magic. It does. You feel cleansed.

Back on the street you admire the juxtaposition of hand–to–mouth street vendors smoking sheesha next to architecture from millennia ago. The mosques stand as tall as the alleys are narrow, their minarets as solitudinous as the streets are crowded. You are struck by the effortless symbiosis between the city's base and its lofted spirituality.

Energized, you press on, deeper into the city. The beauty rising out of the ground deepens your humility.

It would take two fully-grown men standing one on top of the other to reach Pharaoh Ramses II's statue's toes. You scurry inside his temple—for you are but a rodent compared to the grandeur and scale of the temple—and are immediately cooled by the shadow–draped pillars and walls, which boast stories of glory, victory and knowledge. Snakes streaked across ancient papyrus rolls look like fluid Arabic script, dotted, punctuated, calibrated by smaller figures carved in permanent obsequiousness to their king who watches over them with a steady smile. You marvel at the Egyptian habit of sharing, spreading and preserving stories for future generations. The text may be cryptic, but the message rings clear in the enormity of the temple. You put your hand on the wall and touch hieroglyphics that were carved into these walls thousands of years ago; the essence of the story penetrates your skin and rushes through your bloodstream.

Later, you enjoy some moments of sun–setting silence. Egyptian mythology says that the Sun God Ra is swallowed up by Sky Goddess Nut every night, who gives birth to him the following morning, and you watch Ra diminish above you. Now Egypt has turned green–the color of Islam. Every mosque lights up, casting an emerald glow along the Nile, announcing pinpricks of civilization along the endless riverbanks, heralding the start of a town or city.

Cairo breathes a constant dance: Pedestrians dodge traffic; women dodge salacious men; men dodge the tourist police and police dodge protocol and demand baksheesh.

You are standing in the middle of the bustle of a congested, smoggy city, listening to the pure voice of an imam bellowing out a prayer to Allah, eating your final falafel and watching the sun set behind a pyramid, resisting the urge to snap one more picture with your free hand. Your hair smells of cigarette smoke, your fingers taste of hummus and your sandaled feet are tickled by the sand. Egypt is not a "clean-toed" country and you couldn't be happier for the dirty and dusty memories you have inhaled and absorbed during your time here.

You survey the street, now familiar and friendly. You remember the woman with whom you managed a three–word conversation in Arabic in order to use her phone. You can still taste the lunch you had with a Bedouin family a week ago. And you can't forget Samir who drove you through his favorite parts of Cairo with colorful running commentary. You fit in, didn't you?

The colors sinking from above, couching a sleepy sun, steer you onwards—you aren't meant to stay. This sn't home.

Where to, next?

Andria Alefhi
MUSICAL MONDAYS

While I was stumbling towards the 1 train uptown, I had already composed the email to you in my mind. Oh, cheap alcohol. Unfortunately, I had sobered up by 50th street. There are drawbacks to living so far uptown. I went out to a gay bar for Musical Mondays with Kim's good friend Sergio and sang and danced along to songs in front of the giant screens, arm in arm with some of NY's finest homosexuals. I don't know my musicals so mostly I smiled and was busy being drunk. I tried hard but couldn't put a dent in my second free drink. I was already cocked from the first greyhound and yes, it was that strong. I wondered what I would do for 2 hours in a bar this loud, but Sergio and I quickly found common ground: hot deaf guys. Do you remember Sergio? He sat at out table at the wedding. He talked to Jon (through me) so much that Jon and I asked each other, "Is he into you or me?" Turns out, Sergio has a thing for Deaf guys. So we both got turned on talking about how hot Jon is. Since he has never been with Jon I took full opportunity to describe how sexy he is stripped down to his Union Jack boxers. When I moved out I considered taking them as booty but decided against it.

I wanted this buzz to last until I got home so I could have permission to think all the things I was thinking. The alcohol echoed in my brain, causing my steps to multiply while I walked and reverberate while I waited for the train. I felt liberated. I was going to ask you if you remembered when I left Portland? August 9, 1999, 9am. You stood outside with Anais and helped me load my bicycle onto the Volvo wagon roof rack. Do you remember what you said my last night in Portland? You said, "These arms have to be all of Portland saying goodbye". It was all I could do to not turn the car around. I was hysterical all the way onto the Powell Bridge.

> No one has ever understood me, and I have endured this in stride.
>
> Sometimes I would like to come undone and I don't know who will receive me.

Today I interpreted for a stomach cancer patient. The second stomach cancer patient in one week. The irony makes its way through the roof. How can it be possible? This man though was all alone and the hospital was totally ghetto. I already know he is not going to make it. I wanted to throw him over my shoulder and run.

For a long time now, I have sworn to myself that if I got cancer I would take all my money and move to Tahiti or Fiji and never return. I wonder if I would be strong enough to do it. If I can't kill myself now, why would it be any different if I was dying? We are already dying. It's not misguided melodrama.
It's entirely true.

No one has ever understood me and I write anyhow, knowing my words are powerful, but so is the ocean. Everyday is high tide and low tide. What becomes of it?

I won't send this letter because you will have nothing to say that will ease me.

I wrote a song in the shower last week called "Inching Towards Insanity" and while I haven't actually played it on anything, I have lyrics and an irresistibly catchy chorus that I can't stop singing. I want a mandolin or a ukulele in this song instead of a guitar.

When I was 21 I wrote a poem about insanity. I didn't know it then. I remember the poem word for word. Having the words does not equate communication.

No one has ever understood me and perhaps I am not alone in this.
Often I wish I were less aware.
I wish I could say it to your face,
"I am alone".
A lifetime already of being the dancing girl. There was more to say, but I am now too sober and the words went out
in the sobering.
—10/06

Dave Cole
JERKFACE

When you're single and sitting at home alone at 3:30 in the morning, those people cheerfully cavorting in the TV commercials seem even cheerier. If you're also quite drunk then it's hard to shake the notion that you're just a few measly dollars away from joining in their bliss. Add internet access to the equation and just stand back to watch the ensuing wackiness. This is why I deny myself the temptation of credit card access.

It was on one such evening that one such commercial made me suddenly realize, "You know, I've never really given internet dating a fair shake." Truthfully I'd never given ANY dating service a fair shake but the eHarmony guy was just extra convincing I guess, plus he said that there was a free trial. Imagine that! This wasn't a scheme by some multi-million dollar juggernaut preying on lonely foolish hearts, I thought, but rather a kindly group of concerned individuals doing the Lord's good work.

Moments later I'd immersed myself in the eHarmony website and set to work filling out forms and answering in great detail questions about the kind of person I think I am and the kind of person I think I could love. During all this time I genuinely thought I was going to find the love of my life. We'd be one of those cute hipster couples you see on the cover of Readymade Magazine often sharing the funny story of how we met.

Finally, I finished setting up my profile and was free to begin what would presumably be my final pursuit of romance and partnership. Unfortunately the free trial at most of those sites is an essentially useless window to the rest of the community. That's where the SERIOUS love seekers are. No matter, I thought, when I find somebody I'll get a money order and buy a one-month membership. That way I wouldn't have to waste money after I'd already found someone to woo. Better yet, I'll find a way around the fee altogether. Heh heh, poor eHarmony. I almost felt bad for them.

What they don't really tell you when you create a free profile is that not only can you see the community, but the community can see you. You show up in searches as someone's suitable suitor, you just can't interact with them. So after about a week my inbox was full of messages from eHarmony. Messages along the lines of, "So-and-so wants to meet you." or "What's-her-name gave you a wink." It was time to make my move.

I logged into my profile to see that a couple compatible ladies in my area had sent me a list of questions. They were designed to gather info on the things we each had to have in and couldn't stand about relationships, to sort of test the waters before the real contact began. I answered in great detail, outlining with great eloquence my passions and distastes. Then it came time to send my response back to my future love. Instead of a confirmation of delivery however I was reminded that there was one more step, a small matter to be taken care of, before the real communication could begin. A mere trifle, I thought. How much could a one-month subscription cost? Surely not more than a first date. How romantic.

As it turns out you can't buy just one-month you have pay for at least six months upfront. That's a lot of money by the way. "Hmmm", I thought, "maybe later." It also turns out that any plan you may have to get around the fee has been thought of and prevented by someone else. So I forgot about it. As a couple weeks went by I got more messages. Some were of the familiar, "look who wants to meet you" ilk while others were a bit more impatient.

The ladies who had initially offered contact were giving me "nudges" and generally trying to prod me into action. Some even closed contact and blocked me in disgust. I felt like a real asshole. I was letting people down, people I didn't even know were disappointed with or even irritated by me. I had with little effort followed by no action opened myself up to widespread judgment and rejection.

Reading over the list of ladies I was letting down, I noticed that several of them lived less that half a mile away from me. They were in my neighborhood. These could be people I see when I walk my dogs. This was getting weird. If I could just figure out who these girls were, they'd know I'm not really that lame. I wasn't planning to stalk them or anything, I just genuinely wanted them to know that I wasn't a jerkface. Well hell, I thought, if I can find them in my neighborhood why can't I just talk to them that way. Maybe even date them ...you know?

Oddly enough, this whole thing was following the same trajectory as many of my relationships. I got way too excited about something and then refused to completely give myself over to it. Now I was thinking of ways to escape the situation without looking like a jerk. But maybe I was being a jerk. Maybe if I dealt with that then I wouldn't have to use an international agency that had turned love into a sellable product to quite literally meet the girl next door. How about that?

Eventually, after a few months of immediately deleting the emails, I cancelled my half-realized eHarmony account. Who knows maybe I should've gone through with it and joined up for real. Instead I resolved to drink at home less and drink in public more. That way I could actually meet some of these other lonely hearts on my block that were reaching out, virtual though the reaching may have been.

What I've discovered since then is that going out costs almost as much as a subscription to an e–dating service and that single women my age don't really tend to hang out. Hell maybe they're jerks too.

Cynthia Ball
THE LAMB STORE

I was raised a Catholic. As I became more educated, I continued to doubt the teachings of Catholicism until I found myself so far removed from my faith that it was now unrecognizable. Rationally I should be an atheist. It is my secret shame that I still believe in God. That said, I consider myself an antagonistic agnostic: I believe in God, I'm just not on speaking terms with him.

After 9/11 I was laid–off from my hotel job when I received an invitation to do some holiday shopping at the Lamb Store in mid–town Manhattan courtesy of my union. It was a weird season here. The entire city was a wounded hospital psych ward. No one was really sure what to do, how to behave. Is laughing inappropriate? Crying? This thing was so huge it seemed wrong to try to go about living, as if we should have all stopped moving out of shock, honor and mourning. But there was nothing else to do. I did get laid off, which at least seemed appropriate. I was collecting unemployment; riding my bike every day and I had just quit smoking after 20 years. I did therapy once a week and tried to teach myself the guitar. I wanted to keep my spirits up, I wanted to make something of myself and not slide off into some grand frayed out depression. I was trying to be a big girl in the big city and deal directly with my feelings. I was not going to crash, like I always do, and have nothing to show for another year in my life besides credit card bills.

I was curious about this invitation. What is a Lamb Store? Is that a chain? Do they have them in suburban malls everywhere right next to Cinnabons? Do they sell sweaters? My invitation, arriving by mail, gave few details, but promised that I was being offered free goods for the holidays, generously donated to the relief effort.

The Lamb Store was located on 44th street and as it turned out, inside the Lamb of God Church. I can't wait to write my union an angry letter–how dare they send such fragile souls to be brainwashed by the Jesus freaks? If this is their idea of help, no thank you. What if I'm Jewish? Obviously, I'm not, I'm just saying, how could they do this to us? But I can't write the letter until I have the experience, so I unfreeze myself at the church doors. What's the worst that can happen? I'm fairly certain I won't be held against my will, forced to endure endless stories of personal enlightenment, and if I am, then my letter to the union is going to carry extra venom.

I enter the lobby through the heavy church doors. I am certain this is going to be just too precious, this experience. I am given a form to fill out. Entirely too much personal information, if you ask me, like my name and where I live, the name of my spouse and children. I am defiant. I don't have any, is that OK with you Jesus freaks? Probably not. I consider filling in the abortion I've had instead. That'll teach 'em. I think I have to sneeze and I wonder how many of the people milling about will rush to say, "*Bless you*".

There are others, like me, sort of, hotel workers certainly. Some were leaving with large overstuffed shopping bags. So I guess there is some stuff to get. And I want to get something for my trouble. I hand my clipboard back to the man at the desk and he looks it over. Some of my blanks are not filled in.

"Do you have any children?"

"No," I answer, *"was I supposed to? The invitation doesn't say I have to have them."*
I'm mildly annoyed already.

"Of course not," he reassures me, *"It's just that we have a lot of toys here. Will you be doing any shopping for children this Christmas?"*

I rack my brain quickly; I think there are some kids of friends or relatives. I may go home to Buffalo; there are a hundred thousand cousins there. *"Yeah, some."* I say. I haven't the vaguest clue who, but someone might come to mind later and I would hate to have missed the opportunity. I rattle off a couple random ages and sexes for three children and he writes them down on the paper right in the spot for the Shopper's children. I can't believe this, I'm faking having children and this man is a complicit accomplice. In a church. Oh, God's gonna be mad now. I am told to take a seat and wait to meet my shopping assistant, who I suspect will try to bathe me in the love of Jesus for the duration of my "shopping".

A bright blond male comes up to me calling out my name. His name is John; it says so on his sticker.

(Will you accept John as your personal shopper?), I immediately assess HELLO, MY NAME IS JOHN as a closet case. He lisps that he is from California and has four children and has come to New York for four weeks through his church to help with the recovery efforts. That bright, bold sticker firmly written and stuck across his heart is such an earnest gesture, one that would garner smirks from any self–respecting (or self–involved) real New Yorker. Yes, I am from Buffalo, practically the mid–west, but I feel I've lived here long enough to earn smug superiority. My savvy city radar quickly picks up on the source of John's weirdo religious beliefs. He buys into all that Jesus crap because it helps distract him from his own homosexuality. He figures it's more acceptable to fixate on one nearly naked man rather than a bathhouse full. God, I'm crude. What do I care if he's gay? And why would I think God cares? Why do I even care if God cares? The whole religious justification for homophobia is just one of the reasons I'm angry with God. John's problem may seem simple to me, but I'm the one standing here unemployed, with no other (significant, omnipotent or otherwise) in my life.

He asks me to follow him, which I do, into a larger meeting place type room that is considerably darkened. There are some shelves, and on these shelves there are small knick-knacks and samples with handwritten numbers. There are shopping rules, John explains. I am to choose things I'd like: two things from some shelves with the smaller items and one thing each from others that have larger items. I should find the number assigned to these items and tell them to John. He will write them down and when we are finished, some one will fetch my chosen items from a storeroom. I look at these shelves, someone spaced out the items in an effort to make them seem not so bare. The donated goods are of odd and uneven origin: a scented candle, a pad of stationary, a crucifix, Calvin Klein soap, hand cream and oooh, Clinique Body Spray, a deck of playing cards. Where did this stuff come from, I wonder?

John reads from my application that I have three children. I consider telling him that it's not true, but it seems too hard to explain. So when we reach the toy section, I am encouraged to pick out some gifts. Once again, it occurs to me that I have no need for these things, and I wonder briefly where I will re-donate them. The children's toys are slightly banged up and out of date. I take paints that I find later are solidified and a spiral graph, which turns out to be missing some parts. I also take a talking Mr. Potato Head. I'm of an age group that had a Mr. Potato Head, but without the microchip that gives him the advanced skills. When his foot is pressed, he says brightly, *"I'm Mr. Potato Head"* and it makes me smile.

There's a large table that is heaped with handmade sweaters. Among them is this sweater that really strikes me. It is crimson red with a perfect white square in the center. Sized for a baby, an infant, not even a toddler. All of the sweaters are the exact same size, made from a pattern reproduced in a Christian newsletter. Women (I imagine it's mostly women, but what do I know?) from all over America had been struck with that same paralysis and a desperate need to help. But how? And so a hundred women took up their knitting needles and made sweaters for a hundred infants who might need warmth in New York at Christmas. I couldn't take my eyes off that sweater with its bold contrasting colors. I had to have the sweater. I stroked the yarn, knitted and purled, appreciating the craft, the time and work someone had put into it. I could imagine a helpless baby on its back, arms stretched out like a star, its movements limited to kicks and giggles. John sees me admire it and encourages me to take it.

"But my children aren't infants." I say.
"They aren't even children."

"It's ok. You can give it as a gift to someone else." he says.

I consider how different our worlds are, I'm certain in his there are always infants, families growing and expanding. The rest of the country is reaching out to NY and they can only identify with their own culture. *"Go ahead,"* he insists. And I see in him the desperate need to help, to give, to assist in giving. I'm helping him by taking. So I take. It's the least I can do. I have no idea who will fit into this sweater, but for a moment, my heart fits in it perfectly. I feel warm. John and I pack a large bag with these items and wait for the assistant to bring down the other gifts I've chosen. He tells me that the people of his hometown, in fact, all over America are praying for us here in New York. His eyes and smile are reassuring, yet they also make me feel like a fraud. I don't feel worthy of the concern. After all, I'm taking toys for children that don't exist. The place on my arm where my nicotine patch is starts to itch and burn. I resent that I quit smoking and I want to pull off the patch and start again. But I'm doing so well, two weeks without, after nearly twenty years of smoking. But for a moment, I can't remember why I don't want to get cancer and die.

While we wait, John pulls out a small notebook, writes down my name and says,

"When I pray to God tonight, is there anything I can ask for on your behalf?"

I'm charmed. Throw him a bone, I think. It's his belief and I have no right to mock it especially since he is so sincere. I look at him from the side of my eyes and consider my answer. Should I ask him to pray for my fake children? That we'll all be back to work soon? Those are phony answers to an earnest question and I don't feel right. I wonder, is God real for him? And if, through his beliefs, has he established a close relationship with God? Maybe his version is right or, at least, honest and God listens to him. I wonder, if John prays on my behalf, will God look more kindly on me and intervene? My relationship with God is now so dysfunctional that I'm too proud to ask him directly for help. I can imagine him crossing his arms and saying back to me,

"Oh, so I exist for you now? Now that you need me? How convenient."

I look at John and find that tears are welling up and when speaking, my voice is cracking,

"Just, just ask him to help me get through this, this right now."

John nods and dutifully writes it down as if he understands exactly what I mean. I don't even know what I mean.

My lack of true faith in God? The aftermath of the World Trade Center tragedy? My craving for a cigarette? That sinking feeling that I have no job to return to? What? But I'm starting to cry anyway, because whatever it is that I do mean, I mean it with all my heart.

I created the pete's mini zine fest in brooklyn because ny doesn't have a city wide zine fest.

fall into zines

PETE'S MINI ZINE FEST

SUNDAY, SEPTEMBER 25, 2011   2PM - 7PM

PETE'S CANDY STORE
709 LORIMER ST.
BETWEEN FROST AND RICHARDSON
WILLIAMSBURG, BROOKLYN

L TO LORIMER
G TO METROPOLITAN

SHOW FEATURING EMILY HELLER
SEPT. 24   6 - 8 PM

fundraiser for NYPL

annual zine fests

richmond zine fest
san francisco zine fest
portland zine symposium
chicago zine fest

and more!

www.wemakezines.ning.com

WE'LL NEVER HAVE PARI

WANT MORE | neverhaveparis@gmail.com
neverhaveparis@blogspot.com

FANTASTIC WNHP PAST WRITERS FROM VOLUMES 1—8

AMANDA BOEKELHEIDE
JENNIFER VIALE
RAYMOND LUCZAK
JOE BIEL
SETH KAPLAN
BOB SOPER
VINCENT MCCLOSKEY
VERONICA LIU
SHAHEIM JACKSON
SAMANTHA CRANE
SARAH DACORTA
LING TEO
BEN MITCHELL
MARLON DUNSKSTER
LORRAINE SCHEIN
CHRIS ROBERTS
BUZZ POOLE
TIM JOSEPHS
J. BERENDZEN

TJ HOSPODAR
JEFF STARK (INTERVIEW)
CASSIE SNEIDER
ED LIN
LAUREN RIDLOFF
MARY FRANCIS FLOURNOY
ALEXIS CLEMENTS
MARK ROSENBERG

ARTISTS:
NICOLE MARTIN
PATTY LIANG
WILLIAM STEVENSON
JAIME BORSCHUK
ERO GREY
GABRIEL LISTON

LAYOUT:
NATHAN SC

WNHP 9
JUNE, 2012
FEATURES:

JOHN AFFLECK
ANDRIA ALEFHI
AMBER CEFFALIO
MIKE DACAPITE
KATIE HAEGELE
SETH KAPLAN
RAYMOND LUCZAK
JOSH MEDSKER
STEPHANIE SMOLINSKY